Buzzy's Adventures in Online Privacy

Printed by Amazon

First Printing, 2019

ISBN 9781095474815

Soylu, Bilal and Aluskewicz, Patricia

Illustrated by Olga Pietraszek

Buzzy's Adventures in Online Privacy

Includes an index of internet references.

While the authors have made every effort to provide accurate Internet addresses at the time of publication, neither the publisher nor the authors assume any responsibility for errors or for changes that occur after publication. Further, the publisher and the authors do not have any control and do not assume any responsibility for third-party websites or their content.

Buzzy's adventures in Online privacy

By

Bilal Soylu

Patricia Aluskewicz

Illustrations by

Olga Pietraszek

XcooBee LLC

https://www.xcoobee.com

Table of Contents

Dear Parents & Readers:

We currently find ourselves in an era of unprecedented and unchartered territory. Today's children are the first generation whose lives are completely mapped electronically. Their data, gathered through innocent sharing on social media, as well as, through not-so-transparent collection methods, are used in a way that most of us do not yet understand. In addition, parents and experts agree that the future use of this data generated about and by our children is questionable and uncertain.

XcooBee sponsored this book, *Buzzy's Adventures in Online Privacy,* to address the growing need for understanding surrounding the issue of online data collection and children's privacy. As a privacy-focused organization, we want to be on the forefront of this important conversation.

One thing we realized is that books about online data privacy were very limited and only written for elementary age children. Despite the fact that children are exposed to screens from birth, there was nothing available for younger readers.

While it may seem that discussing such an abstract concept with a 5 year old is too complicated or not necessary, we at XcooBee are committed to changing this paradigm. Despite the fact that young children have concrete minds, we know that introducing them to data privacy is important. While they cannot fully understand that people on the other side of the screen are collecting information about them and what the consequences of this are, we *can* begin to let children know that these screens come with great personal responsibility.

We see *Buzzy's Adventures* as an opportunity to help children help themselves in taking responsibility for their safety. With a playful approach for new readers, adults and educators alike, we establish accessible language about the abstract concepts of online privacy that will generate a wide range of topics for discussion. The illustrations will open up conversation with your child, and he or she will be encouraged to discuss their online and onscreen interactions with trusted adults. When something doesn't seem right, they will recognize it and report it immediately.

It is through this dialog that we can instill a healthy engagement with technology. We hope you enjoy Buzzy as much as we do.

Happy flights!

Sincerely,

Bilal Soylu, CEO and Chief Worker Bee, XcooBee LLC

Patty Aluskewicz M.Ed, Educational Consultant

Hi! I am Buzzy the Bee !!

I like to play
with my
friends in the
meadow ...

... and on the
playground
near our
house.

Today in school, I made a new friend.

Her name is Emma.

We had fun playing together.

Let's have a playdate !!

I talked to my mom and she called Emma's Mom.

They talked for a while.

On Saturday, Emma came to my house and
we buzzed around in the sunshine...

When it started to rain, we came inside to play a game online.

We had fun racing carts against our other friends from school.

Someone new in the game sent us a message!

He is a good racer and his name is Foxy.

He said we should be friends!

FOXY

EXPERT RACER

Foxy was curious and asked us many questions.

He wanted to know our names and where we lived.

Foxy wanted to come over and play with us!

Mom brought us a snack and saw us talking to Foxy.

She said STOP!

We didn't understand why mom was upset.

Foxy was our new friend!

He was so nice!

Mom said:

> When you talk to people online, these people are strangers. You cannot see them and you do not know them.

They may try to trick you. They may pretend to be a kid but they are not.

They may ask you for information because they want to try and hurt you or your family. They also may ask you to keep it a secret and not tell anyone.

Oh, no!

Foxy is not our friend.

He is a stranger we do not
know.

The next day in school we learned more about online privacy from Mrs. Owly.

Our friend Ginger raises her hand and starts to explain.

Ginger said:

Our address is 100 Main Street, but we are going on vacation tomorrow.

Oh, ok.

Please keep it a secret I called.

I will surprise your dad.

...but Ginger can't keep a secret.

...Ginger's Dad calls the Police.

Mrs. Owly continues:

IF YOU ARE PLAYNG ON A GADGET OR ARE ONLINE
AND SOMEONE ASKS YOU ABOUT YOURSELF
OR YOUR FAMILY, DO NOT GIVE THIS STRANGER
ANY INFORMATION.

THEY MAY ASK YOU:
- WHERE YOU LIVE (HOME ADDRESS)
- HOW OLD YOU ARE OR YOUR BIRTHDAY
- IF YOU ARE A BOY OR A GIRL
- YOUR PHONE NUMBER
- WHO YOUR FRIENDS ARE

Brownie & Lucy raise their hands excitedly when they hear Mrs. Owly.

Brownie starts to tell their story .

Lucy gets to tell her story.

After we played the game, my mommy and daddy got lots of phone calls.

Brownie loves Foxrunner Cable. We have good rates.

As Lucy finishes her story, Mrs. Owly says:

That's right Brownie & Lucy.

By inviting Lucy, the game took Lucy's phone number from Brownie's tablet and gave it to strangers.

Those strangers called Lucy's parents.

Mrs. Owly continues to explain…

THEY MAY ASK YOU:

- WHERE YOU GO TO SCHOOL
- WHO YOUR MOMMY AND DADDY ARE
- WHERE YOUR MOMMY AND DADDY WORK
- WHEN YOUR FAMILY WILL NOT BE AT HOME
- WHERE YOU ARE AT THE MOMENT
- TO GIVE THEM PASSWORDS
- QUESTIONS ABOUT MONEY
- TO BUY THINGS FROM GAME

Later that afternoon, Buzzy and Emma talk to Buzzy's mom.

Buzzy's mom shares with Buzzy and Emma.

That's great kids!

Remember: If you are online and someone asks you about yourself or your family:

- Never give them any information.
- Never send pictures of yourself.
- Never give them your parent's credit card number or buy something online.
- Never agree to meet them anywhere.

Buzzy's mom continues to explain.

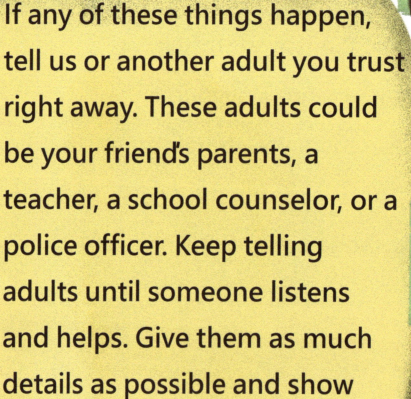

If any of these things happen, tell us or another adult you trust right away. These adults could be your friend's parents, a teacher, a school counselor, or a police officer. Keep telling adults until someone listens and helps. Give them as much details as possible and show them the messages from the strangers online.

A few days later, Emma and Buzzy are playing a game on the Tablet. Foxy suddenly appears again and wants to talk.

The Internet is a great place to play but
we still need to be careful.

Don't forget to play outside on a sunny
day because our bodies need to play too.

Guidelines for Parents and Caregivers

We live in a very unique time in human history. We have more information and opportunity at our fingertips than ever before! As this causes us to become busier and busier, we increasingly turn to new technologies to help make our lives easier.

Each tool we use, however, collects our and our children's data. Since the Internet is largely unregulated and the current laws are poorly enforced, we at XcooBee saw the need to help parents navigate this very complex and confusing environment.

We continuously research data privacy and are committed to the concerns of parents and parent organizations around the globe. We want to keep you informed about the latest information and give you practical tips for safety at the same time.

One of our main concerns revolves around the question: How will the data that is currently collected during childhood determine our children's future? Since website algorithms are the intellectual property of companies, the general public doesn't truly know what is being collected, how it is being sorted and to whom they are selling it. It is safe to say that, at the moment, no one really knows where this data will end up and how it will be used.

Some good news is that the current GDPR[1] (General Data Protection Regulation) laws enacted in May of 2018 in Europe are changing the way people can manage their data privacy and their right to be forgotten online. We are also encouraged that this law includes important regulations on children's privacy.

While not everyone lives in Europe, these laws affect global companies with whom Europe does business. And Europe is taking violations seriously. In Jan of 2019, the first ruling of the law was handed down as France fined Google $57 million[2] for privacy violations. Germany has also leveled a ruling against Facebook[3] regarding the unregulated collection of data across all its social platforms.

And while these landmark rulings are a small amount for multi-billion dollar companies, it sets a precedent. It is only a matter of time before more companies, large and small, realize that they need to look out for their customers' privacy.

As you can see, in our global economy, the GDPR does matter to all of us.

What's even more encouraging, though, is that American tech companies[4] are now starting to realize the need for a US federal law like the GDPR. With the recent data privacy breaches and states like California creating its own privacy laws, companies are calling for one unifying set of regulations.

So things are changing and we are excited that we are participating in this.

We are excited to share that XcooBee is working on creating privacy tools to help with data management for parents and children!

But let's talk more about the current situation in the US, so you will know why this book is important to read with your child.

The Current State of Privacy for Children

The COPPA (Children's Online Privacy Protection Act)[5], passed in 1998, was created to protect children under the age of 13 during Internet usage. Since its release in 2000, large companies, such as Hershey's and Mrs. Fields Cookies, have been fined for violations. While this law was, indeed, an encouraging starting point, over 20 years later, there are still vast concerns about data being collected on children. And it is hard for regulators to keep up with the unpredictable evolution of technology, including the IoT (Internet of Things) and Smart products (phones, speakers etc.). Even if children's data collected is not currently being used, it is being stashed away until the child turns 18.

> There is no agreement as to who is responsible for protecting our children's privacy ...

Unfortunately, there is no agreement as to who is responsible for enforcing this act and protecting our children. Currently, class action lawsuits abound (Disney and Viacom to name two) and everyone says it is someone else's responsibility. Even better, the Federal Trade Commission (FTC) has openly stated that developers need to police themselves, customers are responsible for themselves, or schools can give data consent on behalf of parents[6] . This leaves a lot of room for misuse and abuse by those who wish to gather data and sell it.

Fortunately, organizations, such as The Center for Digital Democracy, are paying attention and filing complaints to the FTC. And, of course, companies like XcooBee are creating tools to help with managing your child's safe online presence.

In the mean time, much of the responsibility continues to fall on the parent. And we know this is not an easy feat. While things change so rapidly, with just a small amount of awareness, more people will have knowledge to take back their right to privacy,

> Screen time for children under the age of two has doubled in seven years ...
>
> JAMA Pediatrics

One thing that must be considered when talking with your child is what can they truly understand at this young of an age. While children are brilliant humans, they learn and see things much differently than adults. Often, we think children do things because they are being difficult or are naïve. Many times, the reaction by a child has to do with their cognitive abilities and what they can and cannot understand at that age. This complicates things when you hand over a smartphone or tablet to them.

Age Groups and Cognitive Abilities.

Recent studies published in the JAMA Pediatrics[7] show that screen time for children under the age of 2 has doubled from 1997 – 2014 at almost three hours daily. In addition, the World Health Organization has recently released[25] its first guidelines around screen time: No sedentary screen time for children under 2 years, and no more than 1 hour for children ages 2 -4.

While screen time is defined as TV, smartphone and tablet usage, all devices are not created equal. TV is very passive, while smart devices allow for the child to interact with other humans, as well, as artificial intelligence. These screens are more colorful and fast-paced than ever and are designed to capture and keep attention. They also create the expectation that the world is very exciting and moves quickly, which is not necessarily accurate.

While the jury is still out on how this new technology affects developing minds, there are many who have concerns[8]. Regardless of who ends up being "right," the screens are part of our lives and at this point, it would be helpful to have better understanding of what children actually comprehend when they look at them.

How Children Develop

Maria Montessori, in her decades of research on how children's minds and unconscious behaviors develop, found that there are 4 planes in a child's development:

Infancy (0-6 years)
Childhood (6-12 years)
Adolescence (12-18 years)
Maturity (18-24 years)

For our purposes and the intended audience of this book, we will focus on the first two.

Infancy (0-6 years): In this plane, the child has what Montessori called The Absorbent Mind. In order to quickly learn what is going on around them, the child absorbs everything in its environment. This includes sounds, language, movements, and behaviors. In a nutshell, they mimic things in order to learn them.

For a child this age, everything is "black and white" and very concrete. For example, when they throw a cup on the ground, they hear a sound. They repeat this behavior because they are trying to understand if that will ALWAYS happen. Seeing the same results over and over gives them a sense of comfort and order in a world that they don't understand. They start to figure out simple cause and effect. And even though it may take an adult one time to figure out cause and effect, it takes a child many, many, many times to figure out each association.

What a child of this age **can't** do is reason to figure something out. They can't think: "If I drop the cup and it makes this sound, the cup will break and then my mom will have to buy a new one and she doesn't have time to go to the store nor does she have to money to constantly replace everything I break and she is very stressed out about paying for things so she is fighting with dad." All he may see is when he drops the cup and mom gets mad at dad. He doesn't perceive anything beyond that. This is how children link things together that don't actually exist and think things are their fault, when they are not.

Why is this important? It helps us understand how children see their world and realize that they cannot yet connect events together to make predictions on how to behave in the future. Nor do they fully understand the consequences and implications of the things they do.

In addition, children cannot distinguish between real and make-believe. Think about when you were young and visited a place like Disney World. Everything looked real. Yet when you go back as an adult, you realize much of it is painted sets. Likewise, if a child sees a person on a screen, they have no concept of video. They think the person is in there, until they get a bit older and they can understand an explanation of how video works.

In addition, when we see a button on a screen, we have an idea that there is a computer process that makes the button do something. And we know what the results of this process are, i.e "Pay Now" etc. When a child sees a button on screen, it is just a colorful rectangle. He or she only realizes it does something when the button is touched and he or she sees or hears a change. And since children are innately curious and want to reproduce what just happened, they child will repeatedly press that button to make sure what it does. They may hear some fun music or a cute cartoon may show up on the screen, and that is exciting to them, but in reality, they have just charged money to your credit card.

Likewise, if they talk to someone in a game, they don't understand that there is a stranger (or a bot) is behind a screen somewhere else. They may just see a colorful cartoon character and all this is to them is a picture. And it may be exciting to them to have a chance to interact with the character. They have no idea that this person might collect data on them, hurt them or charge their parent's credit card.

Childhood (6-12 years): Somewhere around the age of 6, children start to develop the ability to reason. They start to connect pieces of information and draw a conclusion. This is why children at this age get so excited to share something they figured out (despite the fact that it may seem obvious to us.)

You can tell a child of this age about smart speakers; you can show them how a search engine works and then explain that the computer just reads the results. You can tell them that just like we do work on a

> "Children under the age of 6 cannot distinguish between real and make believe"

computer, there are also other people working on computers somewhere else. These people may be good people or they may trick you. You only trust those people you know. And you can have conversations with them about what to do if someone contacts them or asks them for information etc.

So what to do with your toddler or preschooler?

When dealing with a child less than 6 years old, it becomes very tricky to explain to him or her what is going on when they use a tablet. But you need to start at this age when their mind absorbs its surroundings. They can either get a false impression based on what they make up or you can begin to guide them. Then, by the time they are using the Internet on their own, they can make better choices. You see, it is not about shielding them from the Internet, they will encounter it eventually without you, but educating them how to use it wisely.

The next section of this book will give you practical information and tips for helping to keep your child's privacy safe on the Internet. In the last section, there will be a discussion guide that follows the Buzzy story. This will give you prompts to say and questions to ask your child. It will allow you to gauge what he or she thinks already and help you guide him/her in appropriate ways.

Guidelines by Category

The following section is divided into sections by category of product. In addition to an explanation of the current issues, we provide some tips to help you navigate the conversation with your child, as well as, suggest measures you can take to increase their data protection. While we acknowledge that this is a lot of information, an informed parent or caregiver can make better choices about how to incorporate technology into their lives.

General Tips:

- **Read terms and conditions of all websites your child visits**

- **Limit screen time to 2 hours per day**

- **Ask organizations that hold children's data what they collect and why (i.e. schools use educational software, or places that have online services, such as a library).**

<u>Apps</u>

Today, there is an app for everything. They help us manage our lives, allow us to play games and have fun. Apps are a business, however, and thus have to generate revenue. Developers have two choices in how to make money: show ads to users or charge for the download. Since kids can't be charged, they choose to show them ads. Even free apps in the Family Section of Appstore collect user data, and this process is not completely transparent.

You may ask: How do apps know what ads to show? The collected data, which includes the device's IP address, device ID, and location, are used to build a user profile. This data is sold to advertisers and online tracking companies. The companies will track the device ID as it travels from one place to another, collecting a history. This data is stored in the user's profile and used to determine which ads to put on the screen. (Something to consider is that when your child is using your phone, s/he will come across ads based on your previous movement on the Internet.)

As mentioned previously, Google was recently reported by 7 countries in the EU for tracking people without their knowledge or making it clear that they were being tracked. And this is nothing new. Google has been getting warned and in trouble about privacy violations, deceptive tactics and violating its own privacy policies for many, many years. The issues clearly have not been resolved and are still continuing.

Fortunately there are advocacy groups that are paying close attention to what is happening with apps. A complaint was filed to the FTC[9] from 22 consumer and privacy groups concerning Google's violations of children's privacy laws and exposure of children to ads about alcohol, gambling, and violence. Children are encouraged to make in-app purchases. This is still being investigated and in March 2019, two US Senators have taken up the fight[10].

The good news is that some fines have been doled out, including: In December 2018, Oath (owned by Verizon) was fined $5 million after being charged with collecting information on children to generate targeted ads. In Feb 2019, TikTok[11] was fined $5.7 million by the FTC for illegally collecting data on children, including names, locations, and email addresses.

Although some victories have been won, there still is no agreement as to who is responsible to make sure apps are compliant. Google, Apple, the FTC, and the developers all point to each other. COPPA says that apps have to police themselves. And developers can get around COPPA by stating the app is for families. This app would then not be required to follow the law.

As a result of all this confusion, the FTC has a poor track record of enforcing the law. And tech companies are not held responsible for the content, but they are required to honor the privacy practices. The Center for Digital Democracy is demanding that the developers of apps on Google Play must adhere to restrictions on content and disclose if there is in-app advertising and offers for in-app purchases. Google is saying that there are technical limitations to doing this.

Many apps get around COPPA by asking the user for their birthday. We know that a child can create a fake birthday in order to use an app designed for people over 13.
In addition, child-appropriate apps and games may offer the opportunity to login through Facebook. This may prompt them to create a fake account, even if they don't really plan to use Facebook.

The real issue is that Facebook has been found to collect data on you whether the app is open or not. The company also gives data to Amazon and other companies[12] without disclosing it. And considering the security issues that Facebook has had recently, some have decided to be more careful about this app's usage.

> Similar flaws have been identified in other connected toys ...
>
> threatpost.com

Here are some other things to know when using apps:

- **The messenger app, Messenger Kids, is widely touted as safe, but complaints have been filed to the FTC[13] that it violates COPPA by collecting data on children and that the parental consent is easily bypassed.**

- **Snapchat has live location sharing. While this is only to available to friends, children befriend people online that they don't know.**

- **When your child is using a smart device, make sure you disable the microphone and camera for the apps your child is using.**

- **Talk to your child about in-app purchasing. Keep in mind that if your credit card is attached to an app, your child can make purchases. Very young children may not even realize they are doing this.**

<u>Smart/Internet Connected Devices</u>

New internet-connected devices appear every year. While they are convenient and make our lives easier, these devices are continuously collecting your data. Where is this data being stored and who has access to it? Who can purchase it and use it?

When new technology products come out, it is always wise to proceed with caution. Some people will not understand your concern, but keep in mind that companies are very poorly regulated and they are largely left to regulate themselves. And people are starting to question how children are being protected, especially when products are being sold to children, such as kid's smart watches and Kid's Echo Dot[14].

One recent example of an issue with a child's Internet connect product was Cloudpets[15], a toy that allowed children to send and receive voicemails through a parent's cell phone. This toy was eventually pulled from the shelves regarding security issues.

What were they? 2.2 million voice mails between children and families were stored unprotected online. Also data, including profile photos, the names of children, date and month of birth (not the year), and details on the kids' relationships to those authorized to share messages with the child was exposed. The database was able to point to the precise location of the profile pictures and voice recordings of children. The company is out of business, but it is unclear what has happened to all of that data and if it is still accessible.

The issues with Nest Cams. While hacking into wifi-enabled baby monitors is nothing new, the issue is that now the monitors have cameras. Stories lately speak of hackers are getting through the camera's security and talking to people and threatening them[16]. People can see into the room and talk to children[17].

To be fair, the network was not hacked. The issue is that people can use old passwords gained through data breaches and hack into other things (because people use a lot of the same passwords). Automated systems look for accounts that reuse those credentials. I think the main issue is that Google did not acknowledge or warn people against this from the start. And it took them 6 weeks to respond to its customers after the incidents.

Finally, Google emailed owners of Nestcams[18] and gave them simple steps to help increase the security of its cameras.

- Enable a 2 Step verification.
- Create strong passwords.
- Set up family accounts and don't let other people use your email and password.
- Protect your Wifi/password on your router. Use a guest account if possible.
- Turn off internet broadcast/ connection to the manufacturer network if you are at home and are not using it for remote monitoring. Use your own Wifi.

Other Tips:

- **Mute smart speakers when not in use**

- **Be aware that smart watches collect information. Be aware of what this information is and who is using it.**

- **Make sure smart gadgets are genuine, not counterfeit.**

- **Change a device's default password – read the manual to change default configurations.**

- **Don't reuse passwords, start using a password manager.**

Social Media Channels

A British survey of 1200 children, over ¾ of those under 13 had at least one social media channel. And by the time most children are 10, they have unsupervised Internet use.

Many social media channels require the user to be 13 years old to be compliant with COPPA. At first, COPPA required parents to actually verify the age, but apps decided to get around this by refusing sign-up to an underage (honor-system) entered birthdate. Interestingly enough, in 2011 Facebook tried to fight this too, but lost.

As discussed in the previous sections about Apps, children can create accounts, and often do, without parent consent or knowledge. Often other sites, including games, ask to sign in using Facebook. Creating a Facebook account to do this is very easy, and then you can use Facebook to sign into almost anything. And if the child signs into anything using Facebook, this allows for data to be collected on children on any of these sites.

Another thing that we may not want to think about is how parents, in an attempt to share their lives with friends and family, post a great deal of information about their child on Social Media. Marketing companies, in turn, are collecting this information to advertise to you. For example, marketers, taking note that someone is pregnant, can calculate when they can advertise children's products to you.

Tips for using Social Media:

- **Be aware that answers to common security questions, such as mother's maiden name, and pet name can be discovered from social media accounts.**

- **Be aware that tagging a child in social media collects your location.**

- **If you post a birth announcement or a Happy Birthday post for your child, people now know your child's birthday.**

Games

With the advent of multi-player online games, concern has risen about strangers contacting children online. Studies show that about 25% of children have been contacted by people they don't know.

> "...we are urging parents to be aware of Fortnite's features..."
>
> BBC

While the Internet has given us access to unlimited knowledge and the ability to connect with people all over the world, it does have its downside. Especially when children assume that everyone they meet on the Internet is just like them, and do not have ill intentions.

Recently, games like Fortnite[19], have come under scrutiny for leaving children open to being contacted by strangers. While voice chat can be disabled, text chat cannot.

- Talk to your child about signing up/logging into games etc. through creating a Social Media account.

- Play the games your child plays to see what s/he will encounter. Make sure there is nothing out-of-the-ordinary. Be aware of in-app purchases, requests to connect with friends/strangers, chat-room availability.

- Turn off voice chat and text chat.

- Use Privacy settings and parental controls.

- Be aware of in-game purchases being made, such as character upgrades, additional lives, etc.

Video-Sharing Sites

There are two main issues involving video sharing sites, such as Youtube: the content that is being viewed by children and the data that is being collected about them while they are watching.

> "Youtube is a constantly evolving platform and you have very little control over where it goes ."

Today, there are more than 10X the number of children online than 10 years ago when Youtube was becoming mainstream. Children were not taken into account when this product was being built nor are they truly considered as technology has been evolving over the years.

It has been estimated that 80% of 6-12 year olds watch regular Youtube (not Kids Youtube) While the platform was created for users 13 and older[20], children continue to use it as there is currently is no parental consent area. They can also create their own account. In both of these scenarios, Youtube is collecting their data, which as you know is illegal under COPPA.

Regardless of what videos a child watches, the algorithm selects additional videos based on the attached keywords. With each selection, the content becomes more and more extreme. These keywords are (intentionally) linked to videos with inappropriate content for children.

But researchers and parent groups alike have additional concerns about children watching endless streams of Youtube. An informative TedTalk[21] outlines the rising concern between this content and the young, developing brain. These videos get them addicted to watching and clicking from birth. When a parent tries to take away the videos, the child cannot handle it and has a melt down.

One example you may have seen is the hypnotic videos of eggs being opened. (There are over 6 million subscribers to this channel!) Another example is the Finger Family. There are 1000s of videos created in this style. No one knows who is making them and what their motives are. Are they a person, bot or troll? And if it is a bot or troll, what could they possibly want with creating these videos?

In response to concerns of parents and parent groups, Google created Youtube Kids in 2015. The idea was to have content curated for children that includes parental controls and the filtering of inappropriate content. But this wasn't foolproof and in 2017, continued issues led YouTube to create better filters for this content.

> The difficulty identifying kids content creators fosters a 'lack of accountability'.
>
> Washington Post

Some still slip through, however. Peppa Pig videos, for example, have been the source of controversial, inappropriate videos for years, and are continuing to make the rounds. The reaction time sometimes is slow as one particular video had three million views before it was taken down! For every Peppa Pig story, though, there is a viral hoax[22] that spreads like wildfire on the Internet, such as the Momo Challenge[23][24].

As a parent, how do you navigate what's really going on vs. getting caught up in the panic of fake stories? It's not easy. You have to take a step back and wait for the dust to settle. But the most important way is to really pay attention to what your children view. And make sure you turn off autoplay to control the continuous stream of increasingly shocking videos.

But what if your child sees something inappropriate? What should you do?

TIPS FOR PARENTS OF CHILDREN WHO SEE VIOLENT OR SEXUAL CONTENT

- Stay calm and, without judgment, let them fill you in on the details of the situation: how they found it, where it happened, if someone showed them and how they felt when they saw it.
- Let your child know that it's normal to feel the way they feel.
- Reassure your child they are not in trouble. Keep in mind that children come across things accidentally and out of curiosity. Getting angry may result in driving this unwanted behavior underground.

- Depending on your child's age and family values, you may wish to take this opportunity to talk to them about sexual relationships, love and intimacy.
- Problem-solve together. Get them involved in thinking of ways to stay safe online and avoid coming across this content again.

In addition to the questionable content on Youtube, the second issue is that data is being collected on the children watching these videos. This includes identifying data such as contact and location data, i.e. device ID, IP address, location, and browsing habits. This data is compiled and then used to curate advertising.

Considering that there are ads in between videos aimed at children, Google/Youtube are very aware that children are looking at the adult version of their site. In addition, Google identifies its "preferred videos" at the top of the page. These are top watched videos Google that vets and packages for advertisers. If a child is watching videos, Google preferred videos that are aimed at children appear at the top of this page, which means advertisers know who is watching these videos and what to market to them. They have to be collecting the data to figure this out from somewhere, no?

The bottom line, which is suggested by many experts, is to have awareness of what your children are watching. Unlike television, Youtube is a constantly evolving platform in which you have very little control over where it goes. And also unlike television, Youtube collects data on **you** specifically, after which it can market **to you directly.**

<u>In Summary</u>

While this Parent Guide contains so much important information and it can be overwhelming and unsettling, knowledge is truly the key to helping your child navigate the Internet safely. Making the small changes we have suggested in this guide, one at a time, will increase the protection of your and your child's data.

Please see the links in the reference section to find out more information on all of the items cited in this article. In addition, please continue on to the Discussion Guide that you can use while reading Buzzy's Adventures in Privacy with your child. It will help you add meaningful dialog to your conversations around the issues that arise in the story.

Lastly, we encourage you to check out xcoobee.com to explore the innovative tools that XcooBee has created to help consumers maintain their data privacy on the Internet.

Happy Flights !

References

1 GDPR -- https://eugdpr.org

2 Google Fined $57 million -- https://www.reuters.com/article/us-google-privacy-france/france-fines-google-57-million-for-european-privacy-rule-breach-idUSKCN1PF208

3 Germany issues judgment against Facebook --https://www.cnbc.com/2019/02/07/german-antitrust-watchdog-cracks-down-on-facebook.html

4 Cisco calling for GDPR-like laws for the US -- https://www.businessinsider.com/cisco-ceo-chuck-robbins-calls-for-federal-privacy-law-2019-2

5 COPPA -- https://www.ftc.gov/enforcement/rules/rulemaking-regulatory-reform-proceedings/childrens-online-privacy-protection-rule

6 FTC says schools stand in for parents when giving consent to educational software -- https://www.edweek.org/ew/issues/childrens-online-privacy-protection-act-coppa/index.html

7 JAMA Pediatrics (*Journal of the American Medical Association Pediatrics*)

Amount of Screen Time -- https://jamanetwork.com/journals/jamapediatrics/article-abstract/2725040

8 Screen Time and Child Development -- https://jamanetwork.com/journals/jamapediatrics/article-abstract/2722666

9 Center for Digital Democracy – Complaints to the FTC regarding Google and apps -- https://www.democraticmedia.org/article/google-play-store-apps-kids-threatens-privacy-and-poses-other-harms-groups-call-ftc-action

10 Senators propose new children's privacy bill -- https://www.theverge.com/2019/3/12/18261181/eraser-button-bill-children-privacy-coppa-hawley-markey

11 TikTok fined -- https://www.cnn.com/2019/02/28/tech/tiktok-ftc-fine-children/index.html

12 Facebook gives away your data to other companies --https://www.theatlantic.com/technology/archive/2018/12/facebooks-failures-and-also-its-problems-leaking-data/578599/

13 Facebook Messenger Kids -- https://thehill.com/policy/technology/409682-groups-file-ftc-complaint-against-facebook-over-messenger-kids

14 Echo Dot for Kids -- http://fortune.com/2018/05/15/amazon-echo-dot-kids-data-privacy/

15 Cloudpets -- https://threatpost.com/cloudpets-may-be-out-of-business-but-security-concerns-remain/132609/

16 Nest issues Cryptic warning --https://www.theverge.com/2019/2/6/18213956/nest-cryptic-warning-security-cameras-strangers-peeking

17 Recent issues with Nestcams https://www.nbcnews.com/tech/tech-news/i-m-your-baby-s-room-nest-cam-hacks-show-n950876

18 Google emails nestcam users -- https://www.popularmechanics.com/technology/security/a26214078/google-nest-hack-warning/

19 Fortnite -- https://www.bbc.com/news/technology-43988210 and https://www.bbc.com/news/technology-46923789

20 Youtube Complaints --https://www.nytimes.com/2018/04/09/business/media/youtube-kids-ftc-complaint.html?module=inline

21 TED Talk: Youtube and Children's Videos --https://www.ted.com/talks/james_bridle_the_nightmare_videos_of_childrens_youtube_and_what_s_wrong_with_the_internet_today

22 We don't know who creates children's Youtube channels --https://www.wsj.com/articles/kids-love-these-youtube-channels-who-creates-them-is-a-mystery-11554975000

23 Momo Challenge Hoax -- https://www.cnn.com/2019/02/28/health/momo-challenge-youtube-trnd/index.html

24 Youtube Momo challenge video (original scare) --https://www.washingtonpost.com/technology/2019/02/24/pediatrician-exposes-suicide-tips-children-hidden-videos-youtube-youtube-kids/?noredirect=on&utm_term=.e19b40a8d795

25 World Health Organization Guidelines For Children Under The Age of Five — https://apps.who.int/iris/bitstream/handle/10665/311664/9789241550536-eng.pdf

Discussion Prompts for You and Your Child

Much like a book club discussion guide at the end of a novel, we have designed discussion prompts for many of the pictures and scenarios in Buzzy's Adventures in Privacy. In addition, we have given some ideas to help you to explain complicated concepts to a very young child.

Use the questions as you see fit. Since children like to hear stories multiple times, maybe choose some of the prompts during each reading. Children love repetition and the repeated exposure to the concepts will allow the child to absorb the information into his/her unconscious memory. The point to keep in mind is not to scare the child about the Internet, but teach him or her how to appropriately navigate it. Tell the child what to do is a very clear way.

One thing to keep in mind is that it is always a good idea to ask open-ended questions. Since children see things very differently than adults, its good to know what thoughts/ideas you are starting with. This allows you to see where s/he is in her/his understanding of a concept and what ideas to correct or reinforce.

P 7 – 8

Where are some places Buzzy likes to play? What does he like to do? What are some things you like to do when you play?

P 10 – 11

Have a discussion with your child about why it is important that you (the parent or caregiver) meet your child's friends.

Ask: "Why is it important that I meet the friends you play with?"

If the child struggles with the answer, help them out. Make it about you wanting to get to know the other children and their parents and that you always want to make sure your child is safe. Avoid anything that suggests you don't trust the child's judgment.

P 12 – 13

Ask: "Why is it ok to play online with people you know? How can you make sure that you know the people you are playing with?"

P 14 – 15

Ask: "Do Emma and Buzzy know Foxy?" and "What information did Foxy want Buzzy and Emma to tell him?" and "Should Buzzy and Emma tell him this information and invite him to their house? Why or Why not?"

P 16 – 17

Ask: "Why was Buzzy's mom upset?"

If your child is not sure (which may be the case) ask what is on the tablet screen and what is happening there. Ask who Foxy is and why it may not be a good idea that they are talking to him.

Children often don't know why an adult is upset. In this case, Buzzy and Emma were talking to someone that they perceived is nice, probably someone like them and their friends. Buzzy's mom reacted and the children had no idea what they were doing wrong. Buzzy's mom clearly knows the consequences of talking to a stranger online, and it is important that she stays calm and explains the true situation in a way that a child can understand.

P 18 – 19

Ask: "What are some reasons that Buzzy's mom says that Buzzy and Emma shouldn't talk to strangers online?"

P 20 – 21

Ask: "What is happening here?" and "Who is Foxy really?"

The concept of Wifi and two computers communicating can be a tricky one for a child to understand. You have to try and do your best, but keep it simple.

You may just want to say that just as he (your child) is looking at a computer in front of him, there are other people in other houses doing the same. The computer sends out an invisible signal to the other person's computer.

Point out the wi-fi symbol on your computer, tablet, or phone and tell the child that this is how you know your computer is sending the signal.

P 22 – 23

What does Mrs. Owly mean by online privacy?

Answers might be: Keeping yourself safe online when using a computer, phone, tablet, or smartspeaker; keeping your information private when using those devices; not telling people private information over these devices.

You may not feel that your child has met people online or is to young, but you should still ask about it. At this point it may be enough to say that there may be a time where they are talking to someone they don't know and that they have to be careful.

Have you ever talked with someone online? Who?

Did someone that you don't know ever talk to you online? What did they ask and what did you say?

How do you to explain the difference between Alexa/Echo talking and a stranger calling in over a speaker? This is tricky because a child really can't understand how these things work. All they know is a voice comes out of a speaker. If there is a screen with this device (i.e. Echo Show) and the person shares the video, the child can see, but if no video is shared, the child cannot see if they know the person.

But incoming calls happen and just like a child must be responsible enough to answer a phone, the same applies to a speaker. A child may not be able to answer a ringing phone, but with the smart speaker, they just have to talk. This makes it easier for a child to answer it.

To help with this, make your child familiar with the sounds of the electronic voices that may come out of these speakers. When it comes to asking Alexa to search for something, tell the child that this is a computer talking, not a real person. The computer knows information and then says it out loud. Let them know that if they ever hear other voices, they should tell you right away.

Also, if you have other smart devices that have speakers (i.e. a Nestcam baby monitor) let the child know that s/he should only hear family member's voices coming from them. Allow them to hear the voices so they know what they sound like and tell them to report strange voices immediately.

The Topic of Secrets

The idea of children being asked to keep secrets is a tricky one. Parents and friends may share innocent secrets with children for fun, but it is important to let children know the difference between *that* and an adult asking them to keep a secret because they are doing something inappropriate.

To address this, you may say something like: "Sometimes friends tell each other secrets. It makes us feel special when someone wants to share something with only us. But many times it is not a good idea to keep secrets. If the person asking you to keep a secret is someone you don't know, don't know very well, or especially if you can't see who they are (like on a computer, Smartphone, or speaker) do not keep the secret. Tell an adult you trust right away."

P 26 – 27

Ask: "Why do you think Ginger's dad called the police?" and "Who is Buddy and why are the police with him?"

Look back at pages 24-25 with your child. Ask: "Why do you think it was easy for Buddy to trick Ginger?" (Because Ginger couldn't see Buddy, so he didn't know who he really was etc.)

Also ask "Why is a good idea NOT to give a stranger this information?" and "Why was it a good idea for Ginger to tell her dad that Buddy called?"

P 28 – 29

Ask: When Brownie was stuck in the game what did she do?

Say something such as: "Brownie needed help and she pressed the red button to invite Lucy to the game. She thought Lucy could play too and help her beat Level 5. "

The button sends a message to Lucy's tablet and asks her to play the game.

P 30 – 31

How to explain that the tablet took information and sold it? This is hard to explain but you have to say something so they start to understand this innocent thing they did affected other people. A child may not think telemarketers calling is a something to worry about, but adults think it is!

"If you invite your friend to a game, and he starts playing the game on his tablet, the game takes information from the tablet." You can show them your phone screen with a phone number on it. "The phone number and other information about the family on the tablet is given to the game. The people who make the game can then call the phone number and sell you things. Adults do not want strangers to have their phone number and call them."

P 32 -33, 34-35

Ask: "What other information can a stranger ask you for?" to reiterate what was said in the book and "Can you think of anything else you should not tell a stranger online?"

P 36 – 37

Ask: "If a stranger asks you questions online, who are some adults you can tell? and "What are the things you should tell them?"

"What did Foxy ask Buzzy and Emma the next time they were online? What did they tell him?"

P 38 – 39

Playing online is fun, but what are some other things we can do to play with our friends?